The adventures of
Artie the Airplane
and his friends™

I Didn't Think It
Would Hurt Anyone

Written and Illustrated
by
Captain Chuck Harman

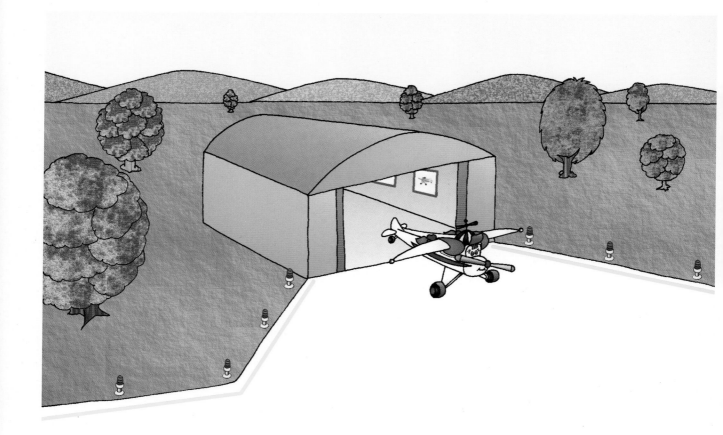

It was Saturday morning. "No school today," said Piper to herself as she taxied outside.

She stopped on the taxiway to listen to the sounds of the
airport.

At the passenger ramp, she could hear the airliners coming and going. She heard cars and trucks on the roads and airplanes taking off and landing on the runway. From her cousin Artie's hangar, she could hear music. "Music?" thought Piper. "Oh boy, it must be Artie's day off!"

When Piper taxied up, Artie was relaxing in front of his hangar enjoying the warm sun. "Hi, Artie," she said. "Do you want to go over to Jack the Jumbo's hangar and see what he's doing?" "That sounds great, Piper," replied Artie. "Let's go!"

Artie and Piper went over to Jack the Jumbo's hangar to see if he could come out and play, but when they got there, Jack wasn't home. "I wish Jack was here," said Artie. "I was hoping we could all go swimming in the pond."

Piper taxied around to the back of Jack's hangar to look for Jack. While she was there, she saw something in Jack's hangar that she wanted. "Jack probably doesn't need this anyway," she thought to herself. "He wouldn't mind if I took it."

As Artie and Piper were taxiing back to Artie's hangar, Artie noticed that Piper had a brand-new, shiny seatbelt buckle. "Wow," said Artie, "where did you get that? I've never seen it before!"

"I found it on the taxiway," replied Piper. Artie couldn't remember when that would have been. He had been with her all morning and didn't remember her picking anything up off of the taxiway.

On Artie's next day off, Artie and Piper were out playing again. They explored everything at the airport. They visited with Jack at his hangar. They flew with Frankie the Fighter. They even stopped by the pond to swim. Once more, Artie noticed that Piper had some new things at the end of the day that he didn't remember her having that morning.

Artie sat on the ramp in front of his hangar. He thought about Piper and wondered why he never found things like Piper did. It seemed like Piper "found" things every day.

One afternoon, Artie and Piper were taxiing around the airport looking for something to do. They saw their friend, Bartholomew T. Barnstormer. He told them that Alice the Air Ambulance was at home. Artie and Piper decided to drop by.

Alice was happy to see Artie and Piper. "Well howdy, you two," she said. "Why don't you muster yourselves into the hangar and we'll catch up on old times!" Alice used to be an Army nurse and she always talked that way.

"Can't you come out, Alice?" asked Piper.
"Can't leave right now, honey." said Alice. "I've got to get
these parts unpacked. You two can come in and help if you
want to."

Piper asked, "Why do you have to get all of the parts unpacked right now? It's a beautiful day—just look at that sky. Let's go flying today and you can unpack the parts tomorrow!"

Alice explained, "Piper, my job is to fly sick people to special hospitals so that they can get better."

"Tomorrow," Alice told Piper, "I'm going somewhere to pick up a little girl who is very sick and bring her to the Big Town hospital for an operation. That is why I need to get all of these parts unpacked now."

"Wow!" said Piper, "I'd love to help."

The three friends spent the day unpacking airplane parts. Everyone was having a great time! Alice explained what each new part was for. That afternoon, Piper said, "I'm getting tired. I want to go home."

Artie looked at the clock on the wall. "It is getting close to dinner time," he said. "We'll see you later, Alice. Thank you!"

That night, Alice's mechanics were getting her ready for the next day's flight. They needed one of the parts that had come for Alice that day. They looked everywhere, but couldn't find it.

Since no one could find the parts, Alice was not ready to fly in
the morning like she was supposed to. Alice's flight crew got
on the telephone and called everywhere until they finally found
another aircraft that could pick up the little girl. They were
lucky this time. It's hard to find an air ambulance that isn't
already busy helping someone.

Pete the Patrol Car drove over to Artie's hangar to see if Artie knew anything about the missing parts. After talking to Artie for awhile, Pete said that they should go over to Piper's hangar and talk to her. Maybe she could help them figure out what had happened to the parts.

Pete explained to Piper that Alice couldn't fly because nobody could find one of her new parts. Pete asked Piper if she knew anything about the missing part. Piper looked very sad.

Piper told Pete, "I took them, but I didn't steal them. I was going to give them back someday."

Pete explained to Piper that what she did was wrong. He told her, "When you take something that doesn't belong to you, it is called stealing. Someone always gets hurt when you steal"

"I didn't know that it would hurt anyone when I took them," she cried.

Pete told Piper to go back into her hangar and gather up everything she had taken. He told her that she would have to return it all.

It took all day to return everything. Everyone was pretty upset with her. Piper knew that it would take a long time before her friends trusted her again.

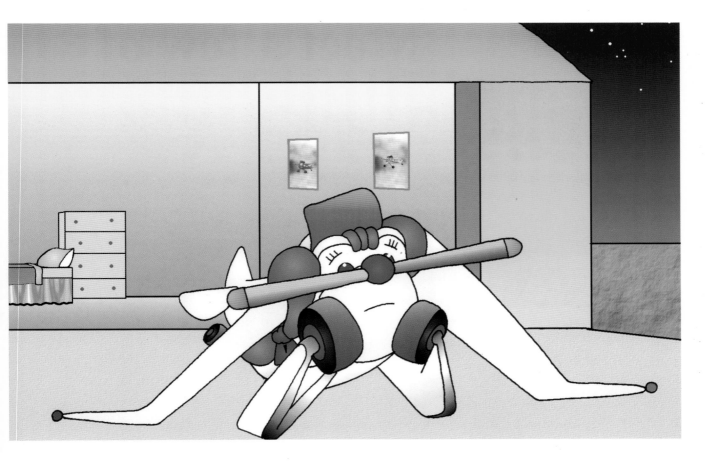

That evening, Piper was all alone on her ramp. "I didn't think it would hurt anyone," she said to herself, "but I was wrong. I'll never steal anything again." From that day forward, Piper kept her word.

Meet a few of

Alice the Air Ambulance

Albert T. Agplane

Becky the Big Tire Blimp

Bubba the Bush Plane

Carlos the Cargo Plane

Codi the Copter

Eduardo the Explorer

Frankie the Fighter

Gilda the Glider

Gramma Cubbie

Grampa Cubbie

Heidi the High Wing

Jack the Jumbo

Jessie the Jet Fuel Truck

Leslie the Low Wing

Artie's friends.

Pete the Patrol Car

Pierre the Plane

Piper

Robert the Rescue Plane

Lt. Sam Sweptwing

San Antonio Sal

Simon the Starfighter

Shirley the Skyvan

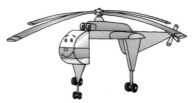

Sigmund the Skycrane

Superslim

Tina the Tailwheel

Waldo W. Wing

Wally the Widebody

Bartholomew T. Barnstormer

Captain Chuck

Artiefacts™

The Wright Brothers first flight at Kitty Hawk, North Carolina, could have been performed within the coach cabin of the largest commercial passenger jet.

A Word From Captain Chuck

Hi kids! Thank you for reading my book. All of the lessons in the book series, **The adventures of Artie the Airplane and his friends**™, will help you grow up to be the best person you can be.

Always remember to eat right, exercise, get plenty of rest and do your very best in school. If you do, you can be whatever you want to be when you grow up.

Visit Artie and me on the net at www.artietheairplane.com

The adventures of Artie the Airplane

RESCUE